# VIET ARCANE

# THE
# VIET ARCANE

Jack Hirschman

REGENT PRESS
Berkeley, California

[paperback]
ISBN 13: 978-1-58790-270-3
ISBN 10: 1-58790-270-2
Library of Congress Catalog Number: 2014939374

[e-book]
ISBN 13: 978-1-58790-271-0
ISBN 10: 1-58790-271-0

FRONT COVER ART BY *Maya Pi Docampo Pham*
BACK COVER ART & COLLAGES BY *Jack Hirschman*
BOOK DESIGN BY *Mark Weiman*

Manufactured in the U.S.A.

REGENT PRESS
Berkeley, California
www.regentpress.net

9v

# CONTENTS

# A MIRACLE BOOK

is what I call the work you are holding in your hands. I'm not referring to the form and/or content of *The Viet Arcane*, but to the existence of the book itself, which involves the telling of a story that goes back almost half a hundred years.

The American war in Vietnam began in 1965. I was an assistant professor of English, American and Comparative Literature at the time, in Greece on a Creative Writing sabbatical from UCLA, where I taught. I was fiercely opposed to that war and, when I returned to teaching in the Fall of that year, I broke some State laws in attempting to prevent my students from being drafted (or so I was told — I felt I never broke any laws but those that served the imperialist war in Vietnam), and I was terminated — ironically enough in the same week that the students gave me the award for distinguished teaching.

Realizing even then that UCLA was a cultural corporation, I turned my back on academic life and for the next 48 years I've lived as a poet, translator and painter "in the street", as it were, first in Venice, California; then in Topanga Canyon, California, where I wrote *The Viet Arcane* in 1970-71; then in Echo Park, Los Angeles, where I began *The Arcanes*; and since 1972 in San Francisco, with many journeys to Italy, France, Sicily, Greece, Venezuela, Haiti, Austria, Iraq, Germany, Sweden, Great Britain, Wales, Ireland, Scotland, China and Colombia — either for readings or upon publications of translations of my poems into different languages.

The only thing I carried out of UCLA, apart from the memories of some very fine students who would come to be fine activist poets and translators — especially the late Max Schwartz, as well as Stephen Kessler and Gary

Gach — was a library card to its excellent collections.

One day four years after I was done with UCLA, I found in its library stacks the book that would change my life unalterably. I had been living at the very end of Venice, in southern California, writing and translating for David Meltzer's *Tree* magazine, a journal devoted to Jewish kabbalistic poetry and prose — that is, the anti-zionist real poetry of the Jewish people. There was a group of hip artists and poets interested in kabbala — Wallace Berman in Topango Canyon; Meltzer in San Francisco; Asa Benveniste in London; Jerome Rothenberg in San Diego, as well as poets and painters who were not Jewish, like George Herms, Dean Stockwell and Russ Tamblyn, the latter two fine actors publicly and in their private lives excellent graphic artists.

The book that I discovered was written in Havana, Cuba in 1964-65. Its title is *A Rainbow for the Christian West* and its author is a Haitian poet, novelist and intellectual, René Depestre.

The book enacts in a series of poems an invasion by the Vodou Loas — or Haitian gods and goddesses — into the southern and most racist part of the United States.

It was published in French in Paris by Présence Africaine in 1967. I discovered in 1970, translated it in Venice and Topanga Canyon from December 1971-March 1972. It would appear later that year by the Red Hill Press of Fairfax, California, whose publisher, John McBride, lived in the north of the State, but whose colleague, Paul Vangelisti, an Italo-American poet originally from North Beach in San Francisco, lived in Los Angeles and edited the very fine international poetry journal, Invisible City.

I've clarified the details of the Depestre book for two reasons: (1) as I've said many times before, it was my translation of the "...*Rainbow*..." book that turned me into a communist as a poet, so it was a momentous eventuation for me, and (2) it lead to what ultimately is *The Viet Arcane*.

That is, a couple of month after I'd completed the translation, I saw a notice in a footnote to a book I was reading about Vietnam that one Maurice Durand had written a book — *The Technique and Pantheon of the Vietnamese Mediums* (I translate the original French), which was based upon a Vodou sect in Vietnam!

I sent off to Paris for the book and was amazed to discover when it arrived that it contained the 24 song/ texts (in both Chinese and Vietnamese) of a sect of Mediums who follow the *Dao Mau* (the Worship of the Mother) religion, whose ritual, which the book describes not merely in words but with more than 50 pages of photographs of Mediums in action, is called *Len Dong*.

Though the sect's activities were banned by the North Vietnamese government during the war as a grouping that might promote superstition, I was particularly moved by the account of the Mediums, especially in the light of its *vodouisant* dimension, after having translated Depestre's book only a short time before. I'd studied a good deal of the people and history and language of Vietnam since the American war had begun. Inspired both by the Durand book, and the anti-war work of the "mediums" of media at Pacifica Radio's KPFK station (my wife at that time Ruth was head of Drama and Literature for the station; we'd done many anti-war broadcasts, and so it wasn't difficult for me to include the cultural workers there by transferring them into the texts), I wrote *The Viet Arcane* over the next three months in 1972 in Topanga Canyon, California.

That was not the title I gave the book in 1972. At first I called it *Len Dong* and then, after I'd left southern California for San Francisco in the autumn of that year, I changed the title twice in ensuing years — to Anh, for one, and Nam for another — when I sent it as a submission to a publisher. That's perhaps why the book was literally lost since 1996, the last year I recall sending it to a press in hopes of publication.

The three copies of the manuscript all had either been lost, discarded or I didn't know what had happened to them, except that I no longer had a copy of the text, and my original handwritten copy had gotten, for the most part — except for a few of the 36 sections—lost as well.

And yet, during the '70's in San Francisco, when I had copies of the manuscript, after having met a young Chinese-Vietnamese filmmaker, Paul Kwan, and given him the manuscript to read, I was informed by him a couple of weeks later that he knew of a temple on Potrero Boulevard where the *Len Dong* ritual was performed!

I was astonished. A week later, accompanied by Paul and his artist partner, Arnold Iger, I attended the ritual. In subsequent weeks I attended the temple once again, and the congregation even allowed Paul and Arnold to film the service. At that time I believe there was but one temple in the northern California area, (and that temple on Potrero Boulevard was destroyed by a suspicious fire and the congregation forced to move to St. Jose). Today in fact — with the lifting in Vietnam of prohibitions after the war in 1975 and the subsequent loosening of laws against sects within and outside Vietnam — temples are flourishing in that southeast Asian country and no less than 11 temples exist in Silicon Valley of northern California!

So it was that the "miracle" — that is, the miraculous recovery of the manuscript — occurred. On December 12, 2012, the day before my 79th birthday, Alessandra Bava, who's writing my biography in Rome, wrote to say she'd a birthday gift for me: she'd found the manuscript in the archive of La Salle College in the Philadelphia area. Apparently I'd sent the text to a group of Vietnamese activists in the Boston area, which, after the war ended, sold its archive to that college, and my text was among its documents. Alessandra had remembered one of the titles I had given the manuscript and, when surfing the internet for material on my life, discovered the texts, bravely convinced that college's library to release the texts to her for me.

What a joy to receive that attachment to Alessandra Bava's email! After 16 years in oblivion! Of course much had happened to me in 40 years (most eminently the loss of my son David at 25 to leukemia/lymphoma in 1982, and my years with the Communist Labor Party 1980-1992), though I was surprised to discover, over the first two months of 2013, when I went through the texts, that the bedrock intuitions and political thrust were already embedded. What I've done here is bring a deeper sense of rage against the imperialism that still tyrannizes the world from its center in Washington, D.C. And I've changed the title, arcanized it as it were, since, historically speaking, my masterwork, *The Arcanes*, published in Italy by Multimedia Edizioni in the American language in 2006, was actually begun in Echo Park, Los Angeles, a month after I completed this work, when my marriage dissolved and I left Topanga Canyon and was staying at the home of Paul Vangelisti and his then wife, Margaret.

This *Arcane*, reworked in 2013, will be included in the second "tower" of *Arcanes* (the first contains 126 *Arcanes*; the second, a work in progress, numbers 108 and continuing.

My heartfelt thanks to Alessandra Bava, for the recovery of the texts; to Ingrid Swanberg of Abacus Press, who diligently searched for the last copy of the text I sent, to no avail (probably because I'd changed the title of the manuscript); to Trang Cao, a Vietnamese-Canadian who helped me with transliterations into Vietnamese of the names of some of my friends. All three women are excellent poets and, in fact, I've included Trang in one of the sections because her help has been like a Medium's for this book.

And to Maya Pi Docampo Pham who, in 2008, at the age of 4, painted the cover that I've chosen for this book. She is the daughter of a dear Vietnamese friend, Maria Pham of San Francisco.

And to Mark Weiman of Regent Press, who understands that, even if my childhood was lived during the Second World War, and that that war is a destruction that effects everyone—even if one were born after it was over—the American war in Vietnam was the major catastrophe in my, and others' adult life of this generation, and must not ever be forgotten by this and future epochs.

*Jack Hirschman, 2014*

# Prologue

We were married
            17 years ago today.
I write this in the manner
            of our friendship
the first moment we met.
How could we know
            our hands would find
        the Party of this love
        and that a people
would bind us to the whole world
            so completely.
Even then, though we didn't know it,
        space was preparing
            this deepest tree.
In the book on kabbala I can see
        the 10 sephirot forming
            the Tree of Life.
But the one it ultimately derives from,
        the tall tree with the children
            burning in it,
            I look at with another eye.
What can one make to gift what prince?
What virgin when these fields are strewn
            with hymens.
I pick up a dead infant in a poem
        and carry him to the next village,
out of the path of the bombardment.
He lives in the arms of my free verse,
            I recognize him:
a burned Jesus Christ of three years,
            our abortion.
In the poem, our

only hope and Party
            he lives,  a fiction truer
than the science of the war
                which murdered him,
this little "criminal" of our exaltation
who's become a grain of rice in my hand.
I taste it like
            one of the thousands thrown at us.
I taste with you
        under the Khan-Phu-Dien,
                the red veil,
        the wine and the way of our wedding
                    in the true temple
        in Ha Noi,
                and in the darkness later
I run my hand over your body, beloved,
                bleeding beside me,
the river outside braiding its hair
        with fire and water, the air
    teeming with eyes that
                stare and stare,
not yet born and already
                not wanting to be,
curving back inwardly,
                fetuses all over the sky
that's round as a womb
that
        refuses
            to ring
for the world will not be there,
        save only by the sounding
                of the poesea.
We die its rhythms, its rainbow
    colors that the heart

leaps whale-up.
And the bridges, so many small ribs.
    The hills we've kept
    to ourselves
        like blushes of breasts.
You taste the blackening chokeberry
    and morsels of betel-nut mixed
with the bitters of friends
        and family bombed,
sprayed to death.
        I taste the miles and miles
of tunnels under the earth
    where we lived and resisted,
where only Len-Dong and the struggle
        for the victory of justice
            could redeem
        the small graves lining
the cloaks of our utter nakedness
        that all the world may see.

# 1.

## HAT STREET

Girls as flowers of
      Co-Bo, round hibiscus
of a face,
       a painted moon Xe-Kinh-A
of the Viet
     who's danced all the wars
       of her horse Ngo
seeding magicians, amulets of oh,
   most incensed fragrant
altars of ah,
       still moist in death,
Ho and Florence Beaumont
  along with the pantheon
of Dao-Mau, the mothers,
    princes and princesses,
and peach, orchid, cinnamon bark,
    lily and fishbone come together
to admire the tiger and snake, all
    changes of tone and texture,
and the unicorn wanders and the male
      phoenix flames and the two
   dance in place 'round
the auras of the one ha-
        Do-ha.
Dong, boy, they've made me
   into a skeleton bone
      on the outskirts.
   Witherings.
I see my skin of wood, wan to

the others.
Island after island — Greece,
    Britain, New York, Haiti, Japan;
peninsula after peninsula — Spain,
San Francisco, the Marina of the King.
            This is
her ceremony of vietvodou,
    here among us Voh-Hinh-Va chews
betel-nut, swigs vodka from the neck
    of the bottle, smokes three cigarettes
        at once here at the end
                of the war
            where we began
            inside her, the Point
where ass and elephant
                    once met and fought
and now lie together in the deep
        victorious forest, all
the animals — cat, goat, dog, cock —
        moving to the spirit melodies,
and the 4 tigers of different colors
encircle
        the Black Tiger's
        growl of triumph in the crotch
of the sky's star-flung tapestry,
            who chews a flaming
            bunch of incense sticks,
        laps vodka from a bowl
            on the floor, eats
    raw meat and can chew glass!
            Ngo
            at the summit
            of the zodiac
            of the human

face:
loa of Yen-Lang-Yeu pulsing with
pituitary memories,
scintillant star chual
at the head of the stampede
of happy beasts
in the human Year
of the Ox.

# 2.

## HAMPER STREET

I said: She, I say as well
my brother
    where I find him
        in the world outside
the impossible atom
we're imprisoned in,
      sublime with revolutionary
                ideas,
shaking hands made of radicals
    and hieroglyphs,
the blood of the trees
    of brotherly love: Philadelphia
where Joseph Morrone published
    *Vocabulary of*
*the Cochinchinese Language*
    the same year as
        Isaac Myers, *Qabbalah.*
Sua-Yet-Thi
    of the paper flower sorceries
written in snowflakes and rice-grains
        in whom in the past only
the kabbalist and the butterfly
    on the tail of the horse
at the phalanx of Fourier's heaven
           could read
the face of Earth
    through and throughth.
Now well-known, this woman
    Medium Anh-Loa-Mau

steadily attends
to the incense and flowers
    at the opening of Len-Dong,
and the tears from the war,
        dried on the stave of life,
become streams again and speak
    of the trees
            nudging against
the banks made of human bodies
                and shrapnel,
and hear hills whisper to each other again
and, delta to delta, the feminine
    tender press of soft
grape-skin under the eyelids
        of everyone asleep or awake.
Wisdom's doves
    flutter out of her ears;
she comes out of the cold waterfall
        and does the Rowing Dance,
    Khoan-Khoan-Ho-Khoan
    rowing and rowing,
            rocking up and down
with the schools of fish
        where the word for country
        is the same word for water.
Hummingbirds of voltage
        nimb her amber-toned gestures.
A singer intones the six
            tones of one word, Xac.
Tambourine and flute accompany
    the whirling air and the movement
of us all along the thoroughfares
        that separate at the southern gate
and encircle the entire city

       like the skin of a cell
pulsing with the lesson of
the protoplasm that is
          Ha-Noi.

# 3.

## SILVER STREET

In blue vessels of incense
    the Medium, Me-Hon-Xac,
a woman dressed like a man
    in trousers and a hat
lined with piastre bills
     she gives out in the course
of her dance, who possesses
       and is possessed
as the red veil is unfolded
    and the spirit of him,
who wrote with one hand
and commanded with his mind
    all the maneuvers
of civilian and army comrades,
     descends into her
who brandishes a wooden sword,
  turning upon her having been
mounted by the spirit of
      Ho Chi Minh,
turning and waving the sword
    in a gesture of victory over
14 million tons of bombs and shells
     leaving 25 million bomb
craters; in one province
      the destruction
   of two and a half million
coconut-palm trees, a drop
    in the bucket of blood
   of the millions upon millions

of people and hundreds
    of cities and villages,
and the everyday that
            for children at play
or peasants in the fields
        wounded or killed
by the unexploded mines will continue
    long after this
Len-Dong ritual is through.
        Now she circles
the bowl of roses and orchids dipped
        in perfume; her assistants
distribute frangipani, litchi, apples,
    melons, bananas and mangoes
to each on the temple benches.
        She reaches into
a horn of cigarettes for one
            and draws on it slowly
as in her other hand, the sword set aside,
    she swigs from the neck
        of a bottle of vodka,
the 2-stringed moon-shaped lute
    and zither and bamboo clappers
            accompanying.
        Duc-Thane-Mau-Thoai
        Holy Mother of the Waters
    around the cell, the plasma
around the epicenter of
        the rice-grain eye of Ha-Noi.
    I say Loa-Lo-Hung: the vivid
        three-pronged
        life of the Flame;
I say Xe-Kinh-A
    in the tongue of the inmost

suns and moons, in the whirling
    smoke of the starry factories.
        I say Anh:
Image
      of reincarnation
(along the serial barbed-wire frets
    of the concentration camped brows)
of
    her young sister, a poem again
            for Ann
  of that time and this time still
      An-Gel-A, the fighting
       sister
the bloody ink of whose pen
    has written off Annam
and its colonial lies
    for the truth of
united
    Vietnam's
        sanity.

# 4.

## SAIL QUARTER

Where even children
        became heroes,
where even wild bees —
    in that war made by the most
        inhumane imperialist
Yankee government —
        were trained to be
                soldiers,
to sting and stop the poisoning
    of the rivers of
Poetry, Music and Painting —
        Oh, My Lai,
who can ever forget
        their cut-throat eyes,
the insanity in their flesh
    as they laughingly murdered
small children with their machineguns.
        Oh, An-Xa-Ang,
        Oh, Xe-Hoa-Trung,
may your braided rills
        be flecked with green
and new flute-boys trillalong
        and girls do cartwheels like
                Na
                    Lo
                        Ta
            Li
                Ly
as old men watch

from the caves in which
they've lived for years
        and in the jungles and on
the mountains. Now spokes
    of a Honda motorbike
is the horse I ride, strumming
    a gentle litany through
the fields. And I sit you down,
        Trang Cao,
        back of me here
and we'll purr and rev and dream
    emunahs of the hills
        our ride writes over,
each turn, each curve
    an uncial gilguling of hillswerves
smiling at the smiling similitudes
        along the way,
everything at sunset
        sparked and flinted
to the flame of love which
    in our country has never
been apart from revolution:
        blue at the root,
            red in the center,
                golden the outward
        of our way.
            Out  of this dark body
        flooded with blood,
    smile-rainbows over footpaths
            float:
Con-Cai Nha-Thane: these young
        cadre can fend off any force
out to harass the village people from
            living freely
            and independently.

# 5.

## TIN QUARTER

Monosyllabic sounds
and a letter
you've written me since
we've left the East
I try translating
just as I've tried understanding
the nature of hieroglyphs:
letters/sounds/ideas,
a word-music of simultaneities
these fingers canter across,
playing a tone-poem on a flute,
blowing a calculus variation
response to the guitar Da-viet is
playing from
northern to southern
Ca-Ly Pho-Nha,
— all the guitars that migrated
from Hue, Ha-Noi, Sai-Gon
during the war, the guitar being
the Viet's highest strings —
putting together, as E-sa in London,
spatters of a water-based
masterpiece of
an abstract blood-tie
black and white.
It's the perfect moment
for clear sound in tatters
to cut loose
like visible strokes
of ink for

aren't we all of us
                Mediums,
        sisters and brothers of laughter
        like Hieu-Danh-Yem
                and Am-Lich-Duyet
                who tear each other
into different states of jokes,
        who are the composers of this
    Song
                book whose lines are
streams lovers travel,
            they who are
            the put-together light
of the Himage
                bleeding at the heart
                of the rock
                at the crux of the roll
of the stone blessing for
            the homage to
            *Alle Menschen werden Brüder*
as parts-of-hymn in the face
                turned inward and away
        from the brute force
                by the daughters of,
        with caterpillars in them
            changing to butterflying
                kisses of, eyelashes,
        childhood kisses on the eyelids
            in that
            the suicided sing
            and embryos curl
                in cocoons hanging
from the Tree of Ether
                all the night-long dawn.

# 6.

## SLIPPER QUARTER

NHAP Red Veil
NHAP Red Veil
     My mother Ne-Ly has
descended into the Medium you
     soon shall hear. She named me
(perhaps for Annam): Jacque,
     which translates: James
in American. Which no one ever
     called me. Only Jack.
A biblic Jacob. I jerk the reins
     of Da-Que, the horse
that's been given me to look me
     in the eyes. A grace and a dignity,
though the earth under us has been
     torn up, shit upon, muddied.
The body stable. I look Da-Que
     straight in the eyes. Bloodshot
from the rains. I stroke the fine
     long muzzle. We stink together
of blood, straw, horseshit, sublime oils
     out here in the open. I pat
his rump. His enormous cock
     hangs down and pisses
     yellow steaming urine in what
was once a garden. A flower sings up
     out of the mud. Two.
     The color of sparks.
Suddenly they're behind my eyes,
     Like two mischievous princesses

asking for cigarettes. I light a path for them
through the woods, the way a singsong
of school away from school is
"pretty cat,
cuddly dog,
rabbits, hens,
loving pets,
our friends".
Lao-Am-Van and Hai-Ha-An,
where we sat and, together, the sunlight
is still upon the swing set,
though it is midnight
and the Medium's fan is slowly being
opened like a codex to welcome
her voice:
"I have no hair. No money. Others support me.
I hardly touch anything outside
myself, am simply there, outside,
in here, otherwise
a skeleton, an empty body, a chair. I have
no clothes but these words;
what I wear on this other body is illusion.
I have no shoulders for
the carrying of anything to the next village.
I step with respectful thanks,
dropping down across
the world's urgent ecologies. I pass through
the lights we've all waited for.
The middle is where we're knees
for the bending toward
the Equilibrium of the Balance,
when Face hadn't yet encountered Face.
I observe now a world
all incorporated and bla-bla-bla-ing

with so-forths and whatevers of greed.
    I am no body. My hands are
       my eyes. Not flesh but letters
of language. More, I have no eyes, no head,
      there's nothing for an idea
    to cling to. And paradoxically
that's the beginning of the end of war.
     Water for the lips of the living dry.
     I'm at least inside-out.
Turned. Burned. Burnished. Finished off.
     A wandering destiny.

THANG Red Veil
THANG Red Veil

# 7.

## TRAY QUARTER

Great teachers because they love Revolution,
great revolutionaries because they love great art,
great artists because they love beyond themselves,
great emptiness because they love the fullness
    of the Invisibles — the Dong,
        Hay-Bong, Hau-Dong
  like gong soundings
        in the temple of the justice
            of love,
    mediating
  between spirit and human worlds,
released from the schools
    of the arteries,
  galloping free like the manes
    of wild horses
        here in Ha-Noi
and in Ca-Ly-Pho-Nha too, galloping
    across the sancroscape
of two areas thousands of miles
  away from each other,
    one where furniture
returns to the trees they were
    hacked from,
the other where
    insane incest
  dies of its own possessions.
And your face changes
  into a happy boy, Yeu-Dau-Lan,
with flute and cap

on the back of
a huffing buffalo,
and shy Ma-Binh-Hot, torn
and flung under so many eyelids.
Manikins of bamboo and paper,
in western dress
as well as oriental,
manikins the size
of human beings
are prepared with other
amulet offerings
for the flame.
Our names upon pieces of paper,
our star signs
and our illnesses
are pinned to the lapels
and bodices,
our names their names
clustered on the garments.
Suddenly
the ground is
one outburst of flame.
Mr. Nguyen Van Trang,
the manikin, is watched
by Mr. Nguyen Van Trang
and his family,
as it burns like the martyr
of his smile.
She's burning there as well,
the manikin of
Mrs. Florence Beaumont,
mother, poet, activist
who, on October 15, 1967,
lit her body as

a torch of protest
against the "dead eyes"
          of the war-makers.
And all the len-dongers now,
   are holding hands 'round
      the dancing flames.
The rice of exploding
          happiness in the nightsky
blossoms like a new heaven
      to read by, dazzling
wheels of childhood
      I find again.
 Xi-Mon-Ba Yeu-Hai
          and his son E-Ly E-De
appear from one of the caves.
      Years underground
          they have been.
Now they too
      join the dance
and when it begins embering
   and soon darkening but for
      the moon
whose halo's the dance
      that doesn't die,
isn't extinguished, it's the Face
      that's left at the finish
          of the fighting:
two braids, two snakes
          intertwined
to symbolize
      the Sea in the Moon,
the Moon in the Sea,
the animals in the Face,
      in the Hands

linking fingers, in the round
   dance of Letters
      read by word/sound/image
interweaving as if
         the dance were
the sewing of a vast
            quilt of healing
      for those wracked
      by illness and disease.
Long lifelines in our hands,
   dazzled by mirages
      of the depths
         of our fates:
the parafoci of souls
   hanging from trees
      invisible yet whispering,
past voices present among us,
   Trac-Trung and Nhi-Trung,
      the warrior sisters,
   who defeated the Chinese
      army on their elephants
      a thouand years ago,
   and now Trieu-Au
      with her large
         breasts on the back
of her white elephant,
   always a flower
inside a cloud of smoke
      rising from the factory.
All around the clock of the world
   our vigilance keeps
         time to, North and South,
in the war the Americans
      call Vietnam

and we Vietnamese
       call American:
  A shudder in the soul, root-light
  rising over
    every whisper, gesture,
every essence of the
      dance. And growing
through the brokenness —
    the absolute perfection
of being perfected through
  the process of perfecting
the waters of this
    irrigation of dark,
secret wisdom in which
    in every depth
there's a sun
      we're ever
  ascending to, having decocted
    the sinister alchemy
of the gun in the Viet
      morning splendor
of Ho
    Do-Ha.

# 8.

## HORSETAIL ALLEY

39: you lie
    with your back to me
as if knowing my betrayal.
    The snow inside you
    a voltage of hurt
in your sleep-awake,
    and as Jack is jokey
    for Benny and your
39 is fixed
   on the children's army
in your dreams of Poland,
    and we know it was
'39 in Detroit, is the pimp's
    number in Kabul,
today it's
    the 39
vowels and consonants
   of the language of
the Democratic Republic
   of Vietnam
    gently flowing
through the streams
   to the genitals
   of this kar-
    ma: 39
on the door of the motel room
   in Santa Monica
where two luminous
    libidos'

infidelity
like blood-flowers
   cure their warrows,
by a lovemaking that opens
   her eyes and flaming thighs
despite the 39 sabbath
      prohibitions,
   despite the number of
scuds fired by Iraq.
   The lovers are drunk
all the sun long,
      tender lust long,
         also with the forty
   save one
         erotic slaps,
the nanosecond duration
   of reactions to which
the explosions within
   their bodies
      are nuclear kisses
— Cam-On:
      "No, Hang-Rong-Yeu,
         I don't
      sleep with my sister,
   I remember her
         and so she is
   who dreams
in me Brother,
   I make pure fire
      of the bones of
   our incest, Hoa-Ky-Ma
Ba-Co-Ti."

# 9.

## WATERPIPE ALLEY

These effigies of
Thich Quang-Duc,
    Chi-Mai and
No-Man Mo-Ri-Xon
        I touch the match
of redemption to,
    in a flux of wandering
            spirits
in here kept, a flint-up
    of a spark of darkness
in the charred bones
        of all who burned
themselves, crying:
        Long Live Vietnam!
as their bodies became
        ovens of the deathless
letter-sparks, whispering
    through the night
that they're of the sun now
    and the weather changes
            into a soft air
in the gutters and trenches,
    in the tunnels and caves:
comrades like Lao-Au-Vai
    and Kieu-Lo-Yem
becoming incendiary protests
literally, who shine like
        the zohar of the sky,
who make the masses

righteous, and glow
like stars forever and ever.
    Oh E-Mi-Ly, only 18 months
when your father
      No-Man Mo-Ri-Xon
sat you down on the ground
    at the Pentagon
      in Oa-Sinh-Ton
and set fire to himself
  on the Day of the Dead
so that his flames would
    expose the truth
of the American
    barbarities against
the Vietnamese people.
    And as others like him
were burning the flag
   and their draft cards,
    shouting:
I put my gun down
    on the table of murder
    and rape
in your conference room,
    White House.
As it was a dick to you
    I surrender my sex.
As it was a dick to you
    and dick could pour
such horrible sperm-bullets
  into the hearts and heads
and vaginas of women
    and children,
I leave it outside my groin…
    Oh, E-Mi-Ly, now

45 years old,
I go like Ho to live
        behind your eyes
as your father,
    Nguyen Van-Troi,
  as Qua-Lat Bo-Man,
youngest warrior
    whose green vest
and white trousers stride
  with bow and arrow,
who walks on earth
    and is reflected
in the sky, who inspires
  Music, Poetry, Painting
        and Chess,
whose compassion
    for all Mediums
is legendary,
  who jokes with brother
    Dien Toc-Queo and paints
his cheeks with red lipstick,
  has a temper tantrum
        with brother Cho-Ham,
and is trickster mischievous
  with brother Rat-Tam-Linh.
Nam-child, with your
        wonder-making soul,
herbage is everywhere touched
  by your magic,
with respectful thanks
  descending from the sky
while birds twitter at gibbons
    happily swinging
  from branch to branch

in the trees
to please the spirits of
teachers and activists
Quan-E Pin-O-Da,
Pi-Ta Ma-Rinh
and E-O Xe-Rop
who early on came out
with the truth
that stirred their
students against the war,
and lost their jobs but
won the hearts
of the People
forever.

# 10.

## SHOE ALLEY

So I have risen sword awhirl in my dance for you,
Tran Hung Dao.
Has occurred the moment when our hearts shine most
We burn our bodies to make our truth most luminous
They killed our buffalo
they tied me up and whipped me
they hung me by my wrists
they poured soapy water down my throat
after I ate they stood on my stomach
they electro-shocked my nipples ears and brain
they put iron pincers to my thigh
they put me in a hole up to my neck
I was tied to a pylon on a road
they threw my mother into a pond and she drowned
they took me to a movie-house and tied me to a seat
and rubbed my thighs with rifle cartridges
they set a German shepherd upon me
they put me in a room with four men
who ripped my trousers and panties off
and stuck a hot iron into my rectum
pus oozed out and dirt got into my wounds
Lieu-Van-Vat was captured and they
stuffed glass into her vagina before
she died and admitted she was me
they cut my body into a hundred pieces
I was put into a jute bag and they threw me
into a field and put scorpions in the bag
and even though they'd already killed me
many times over they fired bullets into the bag

and at any living being they saw.
      O Pip-Hay-La,
    may our tigers and snakes mount
the Mediums so when the beasts of evil
invade the Temple of Dau Mao, they'll be met
by the growls and venom of our defending resistance.
I've sat in the seat to write the names of all
the spirits in our beloved pantheon of defiance.
We burn our bodies to make our truth most luminous.

# 11.

## FISHTRAP ROAD

You are seventeen, not syllables
but the first girl I ever loved.
It was after the atomic bomb,
your name is Si-Ly-A Cu;
you know the rest of the story is
the shoulder on which I lean and
have been for 68 years you've
been helping my sobbing.

For you I'll gladly write a Bat-Cu
to open your eyes, ears and heart
to a lovely form of Viet-Nam poetry
Mediums in the Len Dong dance to
as well, as well as trancing to after
a spirit descends in light of vodou
in the Temple ritual resonant to the
epic Kim Van Kieu by Nguyen Du.

Yes, that was/is my war above all,
the war of my adult life, the one
I fought/fight inside the belly of
the Beast, as surely as hell was/is,
where the ground of corpserations
was put under our poor feet like
the new world spirit of Fuck-You.
Now I'm nowhere near where I am.

Yes, we went diving underground,
singing into the tunnels. Deep roses we

were, for the nostrils of the world
but they ripped out the petals of
our wine, broke the backs of our
rainbows. We lived in shit and piss,
in latrines in the bowels of earth,
heads forced down in an endless vomit.

Now I receive you, Nang-Luc-Khang,
brutalized and homeless for many years,
from having your brains washed and one
arm amputated, and I tell you, Y-Yom-Yeu:
We never gave even one drop of anything
to feed their napalm bomb, let alone
an atomic one! Down under earth
in the tunnels where for months at a time

we lived and read, read even their
He-Minh-Que, wrote in black fire on
white fire and passed our poems along
the tunnels which spurted out of the
blood of rock the stone-hammered ways
of the splendor and vital comradeship
of the Vietnamese language and the people
resisting the most inhuman force on earth.

# 12.

## LATTICE ROAD

Always the
Me-Li-Me-Kong,
     honey river, river of Me-Kam:
      Mua-Lan-Hat,
from the crown of the head,
  the heart's hidden center,
  to the clenched fist
    'round the grenade of a poem,
one syllable after another,
  one cluster of roots
    after another
in vessels bound to blast
       the enemy.
These Spring leaves, green
      and olive, the true
camouflage for our bodies
  riding the holy rivers
    down to the Me-Kong
from sources in the sky
  to tributaries
    forking down the righteous
groin, down thighs of rice
  to the soles of soul founded
    in the Delta.
    Chey-Hut-Viet,
oh, marvelous bridge between all
  Norths and Souths,
lithe slither of snake
  and swaying bamboo,

flute melodies abiding
all immersions and
            immerzions,
butterflies and bees above
        your flowing dance,
swarming magicians whom
    all the Dong songs know.
Oh, serpentine flame
        within and without,
Oh, dancer detached from
                the dance
through possession
    of the war — the banks
strewn with blood-money's
    victims on either side — ,
trance with me
        and receive the spirit
of a dead saint
        as highest influx
as now we scatter his ashes
    southerly, among villages
gathered along the riverbank
    in a cortege of hope
        that the war be
doused in peace as you,
        oh, Thich Quang-Duc,
doused yourself in fire
        and bequeathed a meaning
more brotherly than even
            the detonator
of a letterbomb
        20 years hence at the desk
of a millionaire munitions maker
        can hope to embrace, —

you who'll always share
   that red wine
    with me
  in the Café Barcelona,
 or like strolling the tan floor
  of the So Café in Ha-Noi
   where we first met,
O comrade,
 we're coming through
  the holes in the body
    you laid down,
we're firing the Ho poem,
  we're Brigadistas firing
through the voids of
   the Tao of form,
and we're reincarnating
  you, Thich, and Ho
in all peninsulas
  and islands,
   coming home
with Fidelity
  in the Peoples' struggle
and deliriodendron leaves
  whipping the rocks
with garments of justice
 being rinsed before
drying in
  the incendiary sun.

# 13.

## WICKER ROAD

I wrote you long
    before I lost you
       16 years ago
and then you were found.
But so many had died
      in the interim
and for 30 years
    since I'd written you
I'd become a militant
    and steadfast
      communist.
Imagine! I hadn't even
   written a poem
    in Russian
when I'd first written you,
      or translated
from Albanian, Italian,
    Greek and Haitian too.
Nor had the streets
     of our cities filled
with homeless veterans
   of the American war
with you.
       Nor had
the deathless
    Soviet Union died
and Mat-Che-Ca
    wrote huge dollar-signs
on all the abstract

expressionist paintings
he'd encounter
in houses
and studios too.
In you, born after it
was all over and it
was safe enough for you
in Sang-Ho-De,
Sen-Gio,
to construct a temple
in your apartment
with altars to
the mother goddesses,
the princes, princesses,
the tigers
and snakes as well.
Your sisters and brothers
in Ha-Noi were just
coming out
after years of prohibition
(because superstition
couldn't hold a rifle
in the war),
but so very poor
were they
who fought against
the irony
of your having fled
to the enemy,
how might they ever
forgive?
how can they ever not
feel a tinge
of betrayal?

Yet there is a way
    transcending the bitter
betel-nut rubbed
     into the wounds
of postwar days:
    Len Dong in Ha-Noi!
    Len Dong in Sen-Gio!
Two fans, each made
    of piastres and dollars,
 respectfully
  are spread open, by
Mediums Nu-Trang-Hieu, very
  effeminately in Ha-Noi,
   and charmingly
demure Hoi-Am-Ap
   in Sen-Gio.
And then plucked and given
  with a pineapple and then
   a mango to each one
    in the two
     congregations,
    respectively.

# 14.

## MUSICAL INSTRUMENT ROAD

Like a pair
    of chopsticks
        in the medium's hand
    dancing, as her legs are,
around two baskets,
    one with the 39 heartbeats
of a spirit incarnation,
    the other with the food
of 12 vowels and 27 consonants
    of the Vietnamese language
whose Xe-Kinh-A is married
    to the Beauty of the song
        she sings:
Who will lift these baskets
    and shoulder this pole
along the seashore
        over the dunes
up the Hau-Giang, Vam-Co
    into the Me-Kong?
Who will shoulder this pole
        and keep
        the delicate balance.
The bombs have exploded
    everything, everyone
        is fallen on the ground —
    man, woman and child,
buffalo, deer, roebuck,
    goat —
        but no longer pulsing.

The dikes only half-mended
    as are the shattered
walls and broken altars
    of the Temple.
When a cloud is passing
    in front of the moon
    at midnight
in the shape of a horse,
    amid the plaintive sorrow
    of the war-torn villages,
who will shoulder this pole,
    these baskets
filled now — by magic —
    with food,
  across the Black
    and the Clear
      into the Red River
north, to be given
    to the children
  whose infancies were
wide-open sobs
    and scalding
    wounds.
Now apricots,
    sweetbread, candies
    and pinches
of sunshiny laughter
  as they all gaze at
    the she-dragon swan
on Little Lake,
    and the butterflies
released from
  Yen-Rong-Khong's tears
make for the honey of

her People's lips
and with her linking of arms
in the dance round
the Maypole with Xu-An-Hoi,
they sway like the four
directions of the compass
rose whose home
in the triangle
completes the star.

# 15.

## NEW QUARTER

When we make love,
        what beauty!
When we fist the air,
    our right clench
        means the Left,
means that flank
        where a sensuous finger
might journey to the delta,
        in the Me-Kong,
    with shyly whispered
affections, the butts
        of our rifles lying
side-by-side beside us
    who've come out
        of cave and tunnel
for a  roll
        in the hay of twilight!
The Mediums Rap-Yeu-Yen
    and Am-Vi-Mang
        of the goddess of love
are counting the minutes
    when sensual hope
can take us in like two
        rice-grain children.
They're slowly spinning
    'round the egg
of night about to be born
    as a demon warrior child
aimed at the throat

of the invaders,
at their viper eyes,
   filled with their lies about
            global victory,
   attacking them
      with caduceus bites,
blinding them
   so they might one day
   look their own suicides
      in the eyes
            of humanity.

# 16.

## FUKIEN BOULEVARD

The invaders
    fix on us,
      try to junk us,
acupunc us with
      dirty needles filled
  with their stars of Death,
stripes of hemp,
        against whom,
through incense-inhaling
    nostrils, vodka-sipping
  lips, possessed,
  Loi-Khin-Banh rises
    from the seat
for the dance,
  Dong dance, Ba-Dong.
In symbolic gestures
    covered by the spin
of the fans she holds
    in both hands,
she evoke the spirit of
    the one who chevalures
  the American who descends,
nibbling her pimento
    nipples, into the seat
  of her body where she's
  inserted the razor.
He rides, screams, ghastly
    gushes blood, curses,
      shoots her with

his pistol dead and runs
away.
Viec-Xay-Ra
turns her head
on the pillow
after he's gone
from this brothel-room
and spits obscenities
at the money
he's left on the mat.
She begs god
push her up
a mountain
like the stone she's become,
and throw her over.
I want to groan
but the comrades
order me to go on writing
and ride me
through the Iridescenses
where my eyes
drink in
her deathless courage,
the furlonging beauty
of her thighs,
my rifle riding
along her hip
in punishments of blue
canterings through
harvests of bleeding hectares.
They're ringing and ringing
Cai-Bao Cai-Ken:
O horse full of holes
I'm lost in,

O luminous loal body
    of Dao-Mau
    kicking the habit of me;
O dust world vévé,
    chalk horse scrawled
    on the blackboard
        of the Sai-Gon sky:

*The women of Vietnam*
*are vanguard against decay.*
*The North and the South are one.*
*The ritual of Len Dong is one.*
*Come to your senses, puppet.*

# 17.

## CROSSING BOULEVARD

The stream running
        after the rain
    called woman
a body of water rilling around,
        inscaping pebbles,
rock-smooth saffron caress
    of foam-sleeves,
her neckerchief the twin
        of her sister's.
Sun-splashed is the elephant
    she rides. Green shoots
sprout out of giant boulders.
        Paint me! Sculpt me!
Poetize me! she cries,
        or is it I
    who've betrayed the kiss
        for a tone, for the six-toned
        North and the flesh
    of dragon's blood ink,
betrayed the floods of the South
    for the red Viet buds
        on the branches,
        for blue foetal eyelids,
    pupils emerging blue under
berry-witch-ebony hair
        I fickle around
        the waist of?
Isn't it close to Tet? And I
    paper-thin and burning,

a Medium riding
a broom amid the neighing
    of Da-Que.
Y-Chi-Vay has only to
    breathe
        on me and I'll spark
from leaf to leaf,
        divine characters,
    Lien-He-Chuc, burn myself
into plants, animals.
        Looking at her, I become
            beside myself.
O sister of last night's moonbow,
    you are a rock this morning
        the shadow of a leaf
        is upon, which
        I run my hand over,
you speak river-whispers
        to my palm,
    a reverie stemming
from North to South,
    this chiromancy, this
        lifeline in the afterlife
            of life, first butterfly
of midwinter Spring,
    a fragrance of natural
vision, free.
        My rifle leans against
the tree which speaks to me
        across the garden
        of my infancy,
    speaks to me who
    am not even yet a notion,
let alone a conception,

inside a vision of a
        ghost-boy at a window,
who once upon an interchange
        was a girl: both in me
                rolling, immy, stone:
young Blue Spring,
young Miss Phoenix.

# 18.

## MAM QUARTER

Red silk for the soul
    about to leave her.
  A bird in space, she,
    Khieu-Vu-Ke,
a curvature of pure rapport
    for fingers touching folds
  like a codex in air,
    now opening, spreading
  flame-red wings:
  the bird the soul and she
the word kept gracefully
    — pli-selon-pli —
of the warrior sister
    of the detachment:
a blend of the finest elements
  of the mineral seasons,
    of the clearest water
    for her sense of justice,
a woman general at 23,
  already an accomplished poet —
Listen:
    "You fell and lay
    in a blood-pool.
    They looked with fear
    in their eyes. One
    shouted, 'The boy's
    still breathing!
    Oil! Fetch some oil!'
    They poured it

on your face
and set it afire."
I who am your elder brother,
Moi-Noi-Dem, meet you
again years later
in the Temple in Ha-Noi.
I whirl on my toe
like the knife
you put into your heart.
But come, dear sister,
give me two or five words.
We were brought up
in that house
over there between
the two fingers
of the victory sign.
Now in this karma dance
of reincarnation,
even our beloved parents
are here proud
of our movement across
the landscape. In Death
and in Life they lie together,
and so do we.
Mint is growing on the rocks.
Across the river
the American plane
is plunged like a pen
into an inkpot of trees.
Leap with me, sister of lichen
and the mint.
Skip with me up to where
we were suicided
from the summit

of Mt. Tung.
How quickly we were
reborn then:
our eyelids in San Francisco,
our narrow waists in New York.

# 19.

## COAL QUARTER

Comes Dan-Nhi, plucked;
   comes tam-tam;
comes Canh-Dong
      and Anh-Nang-Yen,
         tympanuming,
   and on the buffalo's back
         the sweet Sao fluted,
      the Ken Bao piping
            the Trong Quan
               vibrant jew's harp,
   the buffalo dripping
      children and laughterous
         squeals.
It's the play of play itself,
      of self's presidium
         of fireflies
      applauding each other into
         sparks that stir up
tonight's tousels of peace…
            how long ago…?
      your hand…
and we went running through
            the haunted…
That man, Cho-An-Ma, was
   very old and wrinkles I have
      likewise become
a stick sucked and a piece
      of paper.
   On it, Da-Viet, we see

69

              our ancestors.
Who else is
              our poetry for?
The Letters whirling,
       wheels-within-wheels,
the untying of knots
       and the permuting
freely as A-Bu La-Phia
              sang in that house
       on a hill in Messina
and then lifting up
       the body of the Medium
              gentle brother
barely 15 year-old,
   murdered Em-Me-Ti.
Why, my son Da-Viet, Da-Viet
       Meo-So, Dee Em, as in
              Dao-Mau,
is my brother and friend
              like no other
       branching across the staves
              of that strange fruit bruited
in the ears together
       with vicious racism
              denounced by the mouth
              of no less than
              Mo-Ham Ma-Da-Ly
       in the great dance fugue
       performed in whirling
              revolutions
              for the eyes of the People
       holding with love the image
              of reincarnation of the child,
                     child

Em-Me-Ti,
in Trung-Va Temple
in Ha-Noi.
O solar
octoroon of E-T
who's also Xe-kinh-a,
pulling the hair
of her brains
apart so the prince
might re-ascend
illumined by the 36
invisible
pairs of eyes of
the anonymous
La-Me-Vo-Nhi.

# 20.

## BRONZE QUARTER

Down from the tree
    house clean as
        celadon porcelains
or the blues of Hue,
her hand upon the silken
    sleeve of her brother,
        Rao-Hoanh-Ay,
      out walking,
      children somersaulting
      before them across
the field, with betel
and jettisoned polyps
    playing as I am
on this Dan-Tranh
   strumming a hymn to
  the rivers
    Red & Black & Clear
flowing together
      to inundate with
rice tiers and through
    nasal tones
  of the air
          song
    sung sang
       hoa
          bang
floating past jars of kaolin
  and feldspar, through
     avenues of water, rills

against your braids'
reflections, paracel breaking
at our fingertips,
the taste of body after
the never-ended war,
the sticky
chandu paste like
opium of spun-silk,
heavy dusk under the eyes
where everything
inward is inclining
toward the slope of war
become
this slope and this one
unfolding a fan
of a twilight
inscribed in antimony
and bauxite, a pythoness
slithering through
the forest and the silicious
alluvial plain tasting of mud
changing into a bread-loaf
by magic transformed
into a vessel of prophecy
for the Prince and Princess
of one mind
with two lotus-pips
for pupils
gazing out at manioc
banyan roil palm giant bamboo
peppertrees lime-wood
and feeling women Mediums
on either side of the boat
dropping tears that

stir up the sea
with the memory of how
your beauty had been changed
so profoundly by the war.
Yes, we cadre now.
We Dong within.
With hands that have looked
into our eyes so long.
The moon and the sun
at each end
of the sky at high noon
on a fair day we never dreamed would be.
And so we bald allover
and burn like gongs
sounding the call
for meditation,
and we die softly like fire
after love occurs as
the adorable bodice of the goddess
comes out of her combs
pinning these sounding rings
to our ears, with aviary
and small things
fluttering and leaping all around
the new forest floor,
with nature's raw law
— bird cawcaw and echoes echoed —
in the jade Yeu-Yen-
Ze-ro
of "a woman, almost…"

# 21.

## PAPER IMAGE QUARTER

Because my breast's
     an ugly blister and
your bombs haven't stopped
    ruining our tissue
     since Hiroshima,
who will marry
    this hanging pustule?
Out of the holes we're free.
   Your sex never again
     will drive human beings
into caves, or woman
     to become Ca-Ve.
You tried that with guns.
    You tried that with rapes.
With holes we're finished.
  The only future's dawning.
   Fill me with what earth
there is left after
    your poisoning
and napalming
  and reducing our mother
to a garbage heap,
    American dream.
Bury me young, brother.
   The dikes will hold.
  After the rains
    there'll be the sun
rising like old comrades
    underground.

There's Hoi-Hoa-Hon,
   there's  Meo-Yeo-Kem
    and Hoai Nha, who's been
    praying for the sun
        for seven years,
and now
        is one.

# 22.

## SALT STREET

Nja-nja coiled under the skin,
  curled, yet having
    already stretched
  and sprang
    rhythm, curled now
as Ve-Viec-Luc. She asks
  whether the placenta
will fall and, if so,
    will the membrane
(that blue eyelid over
  the waiting years)
    be expelled
from the school of the womb?
  By sitting very still
  she can hear the spirits
    — the Dong,
      the Loa —
possessing the air where
  the vessels
    were shattered,
  leaving only this dry
  leaven breaking between
    our teeth,
    the old bondage
of crust and desert:
The Sai-Gon Pathetique,
The Elegy of Cang-Hoang-Tu.
  I'd have you born hooded,
    not a child

but pure snake slithering
in hand, wand for my winter,
        caduceus staff
                along the breadlines,
spirit of
        Y-Le-Hoi
who passes through walls
                to the Other Side
        where propaganda lies,
that fork of tongue
        my own venom dies for
the sting of the truth of,
        here on my lips,
                my shoulders,
                        my chest, belly,
                        thighs,
I'm full of holes!
I'm a flute
        riddled at the front,
                in the rear,
                        in my mouth,
                                ears, eyes,
        raising them up,
                the double-entendres,
        master-
                baiting them — sperm daily
                        whiplash and yowl
                        from Bop-Cu.

# 23.

## EASTERN BRIDGE

In this propane
interval
where two hands join
Hoa
and bombs
where thoughts
used to be
mangle children,
this balm (not bomb):
that the pun on All
isn't Oil,
not like the soft
lave of this nave of faces
around a circle around a fire
of innerlit
wedding guests
who're the Simple
of It,
the lowering of eyelids
within, to
almost a blush,
and intertwining
arms in a folk dance
of Ha-Noi
for the unity
of community
is what brings
killers to their knees,
a commune
passing through earth

water air and forest,
passing through together,
the one hand clapping
another in a marriage
of Sau-Anh-Lua and
Anh-Re-Yeu,
standing for,
still
standing for
the equilibrium of the balance:
all fickle-winged
flying things,
seen or unseen,
butterfly fluttering a
standing ovation
on the rainbow
bridging this decade
in global space/time
to that body of soul-work
networking ever
upward and outward,
greening all occult
waters,
pouring sheer Light
into the prisms of the vision
and the children
of tomorrow
cry happily out:
SUPPLY SACRIFICE TO
CONSOLIDATE, NOT TO
FORGET RAP IN THE HEAD
on their way home
from school
in the People's heart.

# 24.

## TRUNK QUARTER

(The Tet)

Peachtree, chrysanthemum,
cedar, pomegranate,
silk cotton-tree,
mushroom of immortality,
black narcissus,
jujube, lotus blossoms,
cinnamon, prune,
bamboo
  tree sounds homophonous
   with the long-stemmed levity
    of their spreading out
     and blossoming
peonies,
 pulp of the breadfruit-tree,
  shaking coconut testicles
   down at the girls
  from the ebony-tree.
Cats rats toads cocks fish,
  musicians and lantern-carriers,
  alianthus stumps with
   harrows
 under the drizzling and then
the clouds begin to drop rain,
  raindrops writing
  down the windowpane,
  reminding that words
   can come from anywhere,

O carp contemplating the moon
looking at itself in the water
big as a whale.
                    Ear-rings
            of snails,
    villages of To-Tom cards, open
            to chance, and a young
    guerrilla, Vo-Thi-Mo, sitting
                    at the edge of
    a rice paddy, a cigarette
in one hand,
        her rifle in the other
    as a boy on a buffalo
            comes fluting by
                — ccqwak, ccqwak,
                    a duck is speaking
        to children bending over
            the stream. The tinted
            grey pig of Tet,
                with zinc
                    flanks oinks joyfully
        as the prison poems
            of Uncle Ho are read aloud
and two skydiving
    gulls bless two other ducks
        swimming around a lily pad,
            their bills kissing,
        the gulls looping in midair,
seeing the eyes
        of the mother goddess below
            beholding all this for
                how many suns ago?
The moon the huge hammock
        between the trees

all these village dreams
          are contemplations of:
going to sea riding a fish,
    climbing a mountain
        bareback on a dragon,
            chopping cucumbers for Tet,
                blending lentils
and suddenly when
    we look up at the sound
        of the silencer
            we'd learned to hear
and see the guerrilla Ao-Xmockinh-Luong
        bleeding at the edge of the paddy,
            a fistfire of outraging clenches
        thrust up at the raining sky,
            the cry of My-Yeu-Hep
remembering the blood the ink
    of soldiers wrote in
                throughout those days
        from head to toe to name
    the body Throughth.
Crab, it's midwinter-spring;
finch, it's midwinter, the spring girl's
        strumming her guitar,
    her sister's blowing flute.
Altars are waiting
        for the rubbing of palms
            to part their curtains
and the village slut
    catches coconuts in her skirt
laughing to the shaking of
        "those monkeys!"
    During the downpour, dogs
        broke into the hootch

and now the sisters
are here with tears
in their eyes for a rabbit.
These days of Tet,
Death seems to be holding
their hands instead of
their brother,
and the Medium seems
to have gone
to the dogs, when
thumpathumpathump
at the door all at once
he's here, the rabbit!
Their sun-friend. And the rain
is over for today
rabbits have such big
floppy ears, and the children
roll overandover in glee
across the loving ground.

# 25.

## BEAN QUARTER

My black
tea-brew
rich and dark,
dark and sweet
the sky's wet,
Vo-Hinh-Vu's teasing      insinuations
     seducing
       the page

of night with
a slice of
a semi-circle,
     then another
(stirring)
facing the Aur of the sun,
in the tent of stratagems where
in order to return,
years must go
like poems, like streams,
       behind,
in a great inward
insurrection lead
by a great Medium,
Dan-Nhac-Yen there:
Willow, willow, so old
and broken, you will
not break now, you
stand and be egg-nest
rooted with hat, rain-skiv,
tin-cup with pencils in it,

and the blue robe
        so that altogether
        you hang better.
    How old young is!
      And it still cries: It was me!
          It was me!

# 26.

## COTTON QUARTER

Comrade, your hair
   smells of coconut oil,
      your teeth of sticklack
   lemon juice, clove
and aniseed.
     My hand ticks off
   the clicks to the essence
    of the roses you keep
    concealed in your smile
    that calls me
    your red and black,
   brings the flowers
      of your mission
    to my gaze.
Always the secret movement
    behind the finger
   crossed at your lips,
    skin smooth as
      polished olive
   with a voice full of savvy
    street-cry:
    "Sweetcakes!"
    Banh-Com
    Ai-mia-ra-mua-a-…..a?
— Who sugarcane wants buy? —
    who knows the route
   from Ngoc-San temple
    to Ba-Kin Tower,
   that North/South is

the Little Lake,
the open message saying:
Ba-Hi,
the mystery of the South
the North loveth up
going down
to the Delta constantly.
O Song,
how long must I wait
in this forest where
my mind is
"For whom…?"
for the streaming which is
your thigh reflecting
the seven scintillations
of the Dipper,
to hear the signal and,
through the will-work
of thicket, light on
a canoe where
comrades Han-Chien-Xiec
and Am-Muoi-Min
are riding away from fire
and storm fleeing the ashes
of an incinerated tunnel,
and you pass — after
you place your hand
over my mouth —
your basket to their
outstretched hands
which will float with them
downstream
filled with dynamite
timed to explode

when they're out of sight
of the American camp
on the Perfume River.

# 27.

## RAFT QUARTER

In a long robe
    with wide sleeves
        on which dragons converse
on brocades of multi-colored
        animal patterns,
    in flames made of stitches,
topped by a mitre with braids
        of horse-hair hanging down,
    a belt holding  betel,
        sapeks, cigarette paper,
          amulets to be dispensed;
    below the waist:
        venom and venery,
          pulver of pelt,
      fat chances,
          skinny pickens
of working righteousness
        and with black-boots
        with white soles
Ngon-Ngu-Anh and Nghe-Y-Ta
      are the exhumed bones
      of the fighters
    for the transmigration
    of the Len-Dong,
      the skeletons
    that plant, with the vodou
      of the Viet-Kieu,
        — right in the face
          of fascist fashion — ,

the glory-flowers of the Song
streaming the loving
embraces of villages
armed with
Can-Bo Cong-San
despite that headwound
wound the whirling
planet 'round.

# 28.

## BARREL ROAD

Vang-Tranh, or
    what meaning
    can they find behind
all this petal-plucking
    — he loves me, loves me not —
    where the red-depth
(always spring-blushing
        on the cheeks)
    and their long loose hair
      uncoil and,
        streaming, become
      manes of passion that
      ran with
    wild mustangs
    in a past life.
At sunset, we're all
        Thuy Kieu, know that
    we'll meet Dam-Tien
and sell to surrender
      and grow that
    sacrificial enslavement
    to save our father,
    who art
    in trouble with the law,
hands tied behind our backs
    or tying our hair back up
    or going up into
    the hills of ambush
and becoming brides of the truth,
    a nurse like Mien-Bac-Hop,

a teacher like Panh-Votca-Yeu
who open our mouths and let
the afterlife of our previous lives
tumble out — when we
weren't quite yet, were
only eyelashes, not
iridology, when
we profiled our suffering
to spare the full face —
and now that face
comes claiming
— in the life that's coming,
in the coming that's here —
the end of woman's
suffering as a prostitute,
or a nun or a happily
married contradiction
yearning for a home
at whoever's thigh
of melancholy,
the melancholy being
our own because
paradoxically we've already
arrived! O, Vo Thi Mo,
eternal sister!
We've plighted our
Truth
and embraced the ultimate
transformation
of our People.
Wherever we die now
shall be our home,
for all our pasts were pre-
text for this one word:
REVOLUTION!

# 29.

## BOWL ROAD

Skeleton, we share
    Xay, dust-crushed betel
      grounds, for continuance:
Nhi-Mot-Minh descends into,
    — comes down from palisades
and tiers of fire-falls,
        amid Sung gongs —
    the seat,
    her body delicately garmented,
her ears pierced, her cheeks
        rouged.
She wears under her dress
      the raped rubber-plantation,
    memory of the fan
      chewed by the brutal
    mouth of a tunnel rat,
    the lost milk in her breasts
      for her child Yeu-Yeu-Lai
      tucked into death
    under the ground
      at Cu-Chi;
    she's the spirit of
the wordless silence of this
stalk-stirring of a hand
    in a stream
    floating with chunks of flesh
    and rocket parts
as if the tiger-piss of some
    gnaw war of song

had taken everything away
but the hurt that stays
hanging over,
her brow a stave down there
fretting up there with
her People, — this
In Memoriam to
Nguyen-Thi-Dinh, one
of the finest women
in our modern history.

# 30.

## Bamboo Products Alley

In and out,
    up and down,
   shooting from all the holes
whether a neck-deep bunker
      beside a thatched hootch
        on stilts,
          made of Nipa palm
   in Vinh-Moc
      or from a trench
   camouflaged with reeds
        and elephant grass
   on a rubber plantation
   the Americans wanted
           to destroy;
in and out,
    up and down,
     a hole is Hum,
  our life underground
         in so much darkness
        Hu-Roi-Chung went mad
     one autumn
  living with scorpions, snakes,
    mice, bats and diseases
      that spread rapidly,
   backs always hunched,
    the smells of urine,
shit, body odors, festering
      wounds, cooking smoke,
corpses also like those

in Khe-San after
a tunnel rat yelling Du-Ma
tossed grenades down
that killed two Cong.
Mat-Than-Rang made gasmasks
of stolen parachute cloth
to ward off the smells,
some of us wearing
piss-soaked rags
around our faces.
Week after week,
month after month,
with the children as well,
with children even
being born by a single
candle-light
and always and never ceasing
in and out,
up and down
shooting from all the holes
from the North
to Cu-Chi near Sai-Gon.

# 31.

## LIME LANE

I held your eyes,
   in each of my hands,
 Vu-Mang-Bo
 in the often complete darkness,
   "forever," I thought
  before the explosion
  and I learned
  I would need them
to see again.
  The essence of our struggle?
   Children
    without arms,
     how may they
 write a poem
  is what truly we die for,
 throwing our bodies
   against one another
  at any explosion
or when the flame-thrower
   pours down its death.
 After a year down here
  I lick the dust
on your dead sole, my brother,
my baby brother, Yeu-Hon-Ho,
  I put my whole
  heart into
 your reincarnation
  as petrified mahogany,
  or an ebony rock

harder than
steel to Croc-A-Dao them.
Di-Di-Mao, Meo,
Di-Di-Mao.

# 32.

## SILK LANE

Lipstick on the cup
I sip and pass on
a chain of kisses of
jade adoration,
young links
to the larger instrument
of 24 plangent strings
like our 24 Hymns.
In them An-Nam-Vay
remembered struggles
were stroked like
our flesh together
before we surrendered
to the Medium
to see whether our ghosts
could make peace,
instead of grenades,
descend into the tunnels.
She speaks gestures:
Whirl my hair, make a moon
on my earth-mat, eat my heel
with a lover's mouth,
stretch the long leg
of this bamboo so that
the stress of the love-ache gives way
to an absolute desire to
surrender to
the perfect detachment
of Peace.

And so being
gay as a gist of nothing,
          the breathing of hope
     perfecting Bat petals
in flour,
          like I'm a mad mind
     bent, stooping over
          for gutter things —
rusty pipes, shell-parts, bicycle
     spokes, spent bullets —
to fit together into a new hope,
          making a praise-song,
     an assembly of assemblage
          for the effigies,
          for the many Mediums,
and where tones ochre
          to the light of maize
     and the army of brothers
     and sisters comes
out of the camouflaging trees
          and Phoc of rock-face,
     their coming creating
          polyphonic meanings
chasing one after another
     down side-streets of ideas,
the hiding and seeking
          of children, and women
     gossiping about the stevedores
on the docks in this small
          Hang-Ue village
     and our running is writing
and our words are somersaulting
old sages and young shoots
     in an unoffending offensive

at Tet time, year in and year out,
like friendship winning the war,
insisting upon a kiss
of lipsticked lips,
peace upon paper,
lips to paper pressed,
and tongue-tips —
star, holy, letter, bliss, seed, burst —
of a horse mounted
by memory that sees
the human race through.
May-Chu-Yeu:
mud-swacked rice-baskets
balanced on the shoulders
of her whose straw hat
under the sun at high noon
is haloed by a moonbow.

# 33.

## Paper Lane

As Mau-Dia touched
    my sleeve and whispered
        "Lai-Day,"
            very simply
    a child was born between us
        who belongs to neither of us
but to the other
        of the silent teaching
            between us here
    at the level of the street
where only you,
        of the innermost island,
    have descended with me
to walk in the simple splendor.
        Nothing to others
    among whom we walk,
when our arms
        aren't interlinking;
nothing to the relative
    friend of this space of time
    and one or two stones
            speaking,
    or cars passing each other
                in the night
    who've become the others'
        rearview mirror faces.
I mean to keep you
        wherever I go,
    who for a moment has

given me back
        everything I've fought for:
not the me who isn't I
but the I that's the poem
dying bequeaths you,
        abandoned to that night
            originary in you
in the form of what
            modesty is:
                the Clear.
That best
that only the best
        of the islands of the night
            has given,
        and more than anyone
you want, — more even
        than all the assemblages
            of your own invention —
        the perfect poem.
            How loose
            like the loose sleeves
of our lives these fingers feel
            almost silken playing
the moon lute of
        the war's sufferings
and our People's courage:
        you sitting here, Di-May-Bay,
    and simultaneously
elsewhere, silent, as someone
        other, as Moi-Nguoi-Kinh,
            more subversive
        for your being the spirit
of what surrenders
        the emptiness of this life

more to the parts
    others may play
in the coming world
    than any cocktail
conjured by the clench
    in a pocket could,
    or any weapon at a hip.
I've a picture of you
    no photograph could take,
        as someone from whom,
on the other side
    of an incestuous act
        the deadliest slither
            and insinuation could entail;
on the other side
    of the movie, the tiger cages,
        the agent-oranged
            and the napalmed fields;
on the other side
    of the many barbarous ways
        women and children were turned
            into graves of globalonely skulls;
    I feel the light of you
        within me, Can-Bo Cong-San,
so friendly fine and write-on
    down to the streets
        we were born to enlighten.
From the moment your hand
    joined mine in our
    Revolution together
there were and there are and there will be
    triangles, timbrels, zithers and gongs
        spelling each other from Me-Ron
    to Khe-Sanh, I know Ha-Noi is

sleeping with Sai-Gon
from which the city
of Ho-Chi-Minh
will be born,
and we'll have time/space
to comrade the bamboo,
comrade the tortoise shell
for it's an open heart
that makes happiness
descend like manna
endowing mankind.

# 34.

## HEMP LANE

As if a cycle
　　　turned the corner
of a decade and you picked up
　　　your spectacles
　　and a knife to read
　　　the uncut book of the future,
　　Ann-Y-Am, beside a glass
　　　of clear water.
　In the dawn's slants of sunlight
　　we continue, faces aglow,
　　　workers interweaving
　under the tree of Bua
zealous and lusty with hoes
　　　and spades of morning songs
　　of someone, something moving
　　in each of our bodies:
　a Medium spirit, a pulsing
　　of reincarnation,
of a loved one, but even the stirring
　　of an ant, a plant, the vastness
　　　of a landscape,
　undulating rice-paddies
　　of the waveband,
　the whole transformation
　　　taking place
　　at each shovel-plunge
　　into the earth,
as well as when the body
　　of a young woman

like Chuyen-Bay-Va
becomes aware of
her dark olive breasts
as she works in a field
   under a straw water-lily hat,
arching her back as she digs
   another compost hole
underground in Vinh-Linh.
   Or at the bed's edge
at the end of the sunlight
how her ribs skewer
with sex, a luminous moon
of dishevelment,
a braided straw sandal
dangling from her instep.
All these things you
must do and be, dear sister,
at once all six ways
and like almost never quite
   exactly double:
Nghi-Nghe-Ngha-Ngho-Ngu-Nga
interchangeable with
the eternal fields in the sun
one day male and female
each according to the need
for the Spirit under the eyelids.
And so, my sister, we leap
hand in hand with a joy
the day before tomorrow, when
we already know after
36 years of deep poverty
and gradually then
blossoming reconstruction,
   it will be April 30, 1975.

# 35.

## Chicken Lane

The dead of night trains
    its eyes
  once men and women
    once children
  were hauled off dead
 in the silence
   and the night all day
the iron kept rolling,
  Ra-Anh-Hung,
through the body magneto.
  Now it's the body
    of heavy made light,
it's the the
    — repeated repeated
 on the almost unbelieving
tongue —
    train's eyes
   nearing the end of the tunnel
— no more the crawling on knees,
  burst fingers of a hand
   eaten for breakfast
  in the day drones, no longer
   a taste of the inhuman
  Death we ate and Death we
   slept and Death our bread
   and mouth and hand —
where now
   we see the light up ahead,
    Yen-Binh-Ma,

and it's the literal
sun
blazing on the signing of
the victory we're
shaking and sobbing
uncontrollably over.

# 36.

## LEATHER PLACE

This very clear day
    when we breathe in
      the glory of being
united North & South
    and as a People
today, April 30,
    Hoy-Y-Y!
when the Americans
    leave Vietnam in defeat,
the same date their first
    president, Washington,
was inaugurated in 1779,
the same date Hitler
    committed suicide
    in his Berlin bunker,
and high above
    the rice-fields, fish-grass
    and tench, under the sign
    of the Peach Blossom,
(for I don't know where
    I shall Giang-Dong again,
    — perhaps amid the Viet-Kieu —
    but peach blossoms still
blush in the east wind
    moving through cassia shrubs
    and sophoras)
    my wings glide,
    dear My-Van-Mat,
    in a splendid span,

and descend into
the body of the song
sounding out of the mouth
of the future
mounted and galloping
with whinney-neigh-
heighs, alive. A live
Ho.

# ABOUT THE AUTHOR

Jack Hirschman was born in 1933 in New York City and grew up in The Bronx. A copyboy with the Associated Press in New York, his first brush with fame came from a letter Ernest Hemingway wrote to him, published after Hemingway's death as "A Letter to a Young Writer." He was a popular and innovative professor at UCLA in the 1970s, before he was fired for his anti-war activities. Hirschman is a member of the League of Revolutionaries for a New America (LRNA), a founding member of the Revolutionary Poets Brigade and the World Poetry Movement, the fourth emeritus poet of the city of San Francisco, and poet in residence with the Friends of the San Francisco Public Library.

*Jack Hirschman signing books during his 80th birthday at the Emerald Tablet.*　Photo by Judy Golden